How To Use This Study Guide

This five-lesson study guide corresponds to *"The Spirit-Filled Life" With Rick Renner* (**Renner TV**). Each lesson in this study guide covers a topic that is addressed during the program series, with questions and references supplied to draw you deeper into your own private study of the Scriptures on this subject.

To derive the most benefit from this study guide, consider the following:

First, watch or listen to the program prior to working through the corresponding lesson in this guide. (Programs can also be viewed at **renner.org** by clicking on the Media/Archives links or on our Renner Ministries YouTube channel.)

Second, take the time to look up the scriptures included in each lesson. Prayerfully consider their application to your own life.

Third, use a journal or notebook to make note of your answers to each lesson's Study Questions and Practical Application challenges.

Fourth, invest specific time in prayer and in the Word of God to consult with the Holy Spirit. Write down the scriptures or insights He reveals to you.

Finally, take action! Whatever the Lord tells you to do according to His Word, do it.

For added insights on this subject, it is recommended that you obtain *My Spirit-Empowered Day — A Sparkling Gems from the Greek Guided Devotional Journal.* You may also select from Rick's other available resources by placing your order at **renner.org** or by calling 1-800-742-5593.

TOPIC

Do You Excuse Your Ignorance?

SCRIPTURES

1. **Isaiah 64:4** — ...Men have not heard, nor perceived by the ear, neither hath the eye seen, O God, beside thee, what he hath prepared for him that waiteth for him.

2. **John 16:13** — Howbeit when he, the Spirit of truth, is come, he will guide you into all truth: for he shall not speak of himself; but whatsoever he shall hear, that shall he speak: and he will shew you things to come.

3. **1 Corinthians 2:9** — But as it is written, Eye hath not seen, nor ear heard, neither have entered into the heart of man, the things which God hath prepared for them that love him.

4. **1 Corinthians 2:10** — But God hath revealed them unto us by his Spirit....

GREEK WORDS

1. "prepared" — ἕτοιμος (*hetoimos*): carries the idea of readiness; depicts a state of preparedness

2. "revealed" — ἀποκαλύπτω (*apokalupto*): a compound of the words ἀπο (apo) and καλύπτω kalupto; the word ἀπο (apo) means away, and καλύπτω (kalupto) is the Greek word for a veil, a curtain, or a covering; as a compound, ἀποκαλύπτω (apokalupto) describes an unveiling; a sudden revealing; it refers to something that has been veiled or hidden, but then becomes clear and visible to the mind or eye

3. "shew" — ἀναγγέλλω (*anangello*): a vivid showing or pronouncing of events; to declare; to make clear; to clearly and vividly portray

SYNOPSIS

The five lessons in this study on *The Spirit-Filled Life* will focus on the following topics:

- Do You Excuse Your Ignorance?

A Note From Rick Renner

I am on a personal quest to see a "revival of the Bible" so people can establish their lives on a firm foundation that will stand strong and endure the test as end-time storm winds begin to intensify.

In order to experience a revival of the Bible in your personal life, it is important to take time each day to read, receive, and apply its truths to your life. James tells us that if we will continue in the perfect law of liberty — refusing to be forgetful hearers, but determined to be doers — we will be blessed in our ways. As you watch or listen to the programs in this series and work through this corresponding study guide, I trust you will search the Scriptures and allow the Holy Spirit to help you hear something new from God's Word that applies specifically to your life. I encourage you to be a doer of the Word He reveals to you. Whatever the cost, I assure you — it will be worth it.

> Thy words were found, and I did eat them;
> and thy word was unto me the joy and rejoicing of mine heart:
> for I am called by thy name, O Lord God of hosts.
> — Jeremiah 15:16

Your brother and friend in Jesus Christ,

Rick Renner

The Spirit-Filled Life

- Is God's Insignia on You?
- What If the Spirit Isn't Leading?
- Where Are Divine Revelations From?
- Is the Wind of God Moving You?

The emphasis of this lesson:

One of the many blessings of the Spirit-filled life is the Holy Spirit's ministry of revealing the fullness of God's plan for us. He makes our path clear and shows us things to come. When we got saved, the Holy Spirit came to abide within us. We stepped into the Spirit-filled life, and the day of ignorance ended. We don't have to *wonder* what to do, because the Holy Spirit shows us the details of the marvelous plan God has meticulously prepared for us to walk in!

You Can Know the Will of God

Many Christians don't realize what a rich blessing it is to live the Spirit-filled life that God has ordained for us. Rick shared on the program that as he was growing up, he didn't understand the Spirit-filled life. He didn't know he could have fellowship and partnership with the Holy Spirit, or that he could explicitly know the will of God — until his life was changed when he was filled with the Holy Spirit in 1974.

And over the years, he has discovered from reading millions of letters sent to RENNER Ministries that people want to know one thing: "What is God's will for my life?" People wonder, *What job am I supposed to take? Should I marry this person, or does God have someone else for me? What does God want me to do financially?* People have so many questions, and finding the will of God can seem so difficult for them. But in the Spirit-filled life, the Holy Spirit speaks to us all the time. He reveals to us what we need to know. He even prophetically speaks to us about the future.

You may have heard someone say, "You can't always know the will of God." But friend, that is not the truth. You *can* know the will of God! This is part of the Spirit-filled life. The Holy Spirit, as your partner, wants to reveal the will of God to you. But, unfortunately, people often quote First Corinthians 2:9 wrongly. This verse declares:

But as it is written, Eye hath not seen, nor ear heard, neither have entered into the heart of man, the things which God hath prepared for them that love him.

The very end of this verse emphasizes that *God has prepared wonderful things for you* — and He has! God has been meticulously working out a plan for your life that He had in mind before the foundation of the world. His plan includes everything He wants to do in your life, including what job you're to have, what gifts He has placed inside you, who you're to marry, and what you're called to do with your life. God has a plan *exactly for you.*

God Has *Already* Prepared Your Life's Plan

Notice that the end of First Corinthians 2:9 says God "prepared" a plan for us. The word "prepared" in Greek is *hetoimos*, which conveys the idea of *readiness* or *something that is fully prepared*. It depicts *a state of preparedness.* God has *already* prepared His plan for us. Now, we just need to find it and step into it. God has readied all these wonderful things for us. And if God has prepared them for us, then He intends for us to see, hear, and understand them.

Yet some use this verse as an excuse for ignorance. Some people say, "You can't always know what kind of job you're supposed to take. You're not always going to know what God has in mind for you. Just like the Bible says, 'Eye hath not seen, nor ear heard, neither have entered into the heart of man, the things which God hath prepared for them that love him.'"

Friend, this is an incorrect application of First Corinthians 2:9. Yes, there indeed was a time when no eye had seen, no ear had heard, and the heart couldn't imagine the things that God has prepared for us. The apostle Paul was quoting from Isaiah 64:4, which says:

…Men have not heard, nor perceived by the ear, neither hath the eye seen, O God, beside thee, what he hath prepared for him that waiteth for him.

Under the Old Covenant, people didn't have a relationship with the Holy Spirit. The prophet Isaiah was bemoaning the fact that God had prepared such wonderful things, but they seemed to have a hard time figuring out what they were. It was a time of ignorance.

But now we are under the New Covenant! When we got saved, the Holy Spirit came into our life. We stepped into the Spirit-filled life, and the day of ignorance was over. We're no longer living in the time when the eye can't see, the ear can't hear, and the heart can't imagine. In fact, First Corinthians 2:10 goes on to add, "But God hath revealed them unto us by his Spirit...."

God Makes Your Path Clear

God has uncovered the things we previously couldn't see, hear, or understand. He has made plain all the wonderful things He has prepared for us. Yes, there was a time when we couldn't find those things, but First Corinthians 2:10 emphasizes that God has "revealed them unto us *by his Spirit*...."

Wow! This means now we can see. We can hear. Now we can know. God *wants* us to see. He desires for us to comprehend all the wonderful things He has planned for us, including His will for our life. According to verse ten, He has "revealed them...."

The word "revealed" is the Greek word *apokalupto*, a compound of the words *apo*, which means *away*, and the word *kalupto*, which is the Greek word for *a veil, a curtain*, or *a covering*. When *apo* and *kalupto* are compounded, they form the word *apokalupto*. And *apokalupto* literally means *to remove the veil*, or *to remove the curtain* so you can see what is on the other side. It refers to *something that has been veiled or hidden but then becomes clear or visible to the mind or eye.*

Rick shared on the program a memory from his childhood that helps bring the meaning of the word "revealed" to life.

When I was growing up, we had a large picture window in our house. The curtains were often closed, and we couldn't see the view on the other side. What was on the other side was there all along, but we couldn't see it or enjoy it because the curtains were closed. But when my precious mother would pull the curtains apart, suddenly, what was invisible to us became visible. When the curtains parted... *Wow!* Everything was there all along, but our view was obstructed. And when the curtains were pulled apart, we could clearly see everything that was just outside that big picture window in our house. The view was so magnificent.

Rick went on to describe another event in his life that illustrates the word "revealed" in a tangible way.

> One time I was in Jerusalem with my team, filming TV programs. During that whole week, I had the curtains closed in my hotel room. Every day when I came back from filming, I worked and worked, which is my way of living. But on the last day, when it was time for us to check out of the hotel, I had a thought: *I wonder what's outside this window. I've never opened the curtains.*
>
> And when I opened the curtains, I could hardly believe what I saw. *The view was so magnificent!* It was a panoramic view of the city of Jerusalem, and it had been outside my window all that time. But because I'd never opened the curtains, I had never seen it.

The Holy Spirit Will Make God's Plan Known to You

God has prepared wonderful things for you. He has a wonderful plan for you that encompasses all parts of life — career, marriage and children, relationships, and ministry. According to First Corinthians 2:9, He has arranged so many blessings for you, and the Greek wording here indicates He has put *meticulous planning* into the wonderful things He has prepared for your life.

But you can't see His plan by yourself. You can't figure it out by yourself. Your eye can't see it, your ear can't hear it, and your heart can't figure it out. However, God reveals it to you *by His Spirit.* When you ask the Holy Spirit to help you, He pulls the curtain apart so you can clearly see what God wants you to do.

Through the Holy Spirit, you can see who God wants you to marry. You can discern the job that you are to take and the place where you're meant to live. You're able to identify the church He would have you attend. When the Holy Spirit works with you, He removes the blinders and enables you to see what previously you were not able to see on your own. On the program, Rick shared another example of how the Holy Spirit helps you clearly see God's path for your life:

> I remember the time I got my first pair of glasses. I went to the medical center, they took me in, and I tried on glasses. When they finally gave me my prescription, I was sitting near a window. Outside was a beautiful tree. When they put the glasses on me

and I looked out the window, I could see the leaves of the tree. Until that time, I hadn't realized everything had been a blur to me — because I had always lived with a blur.

Some people live like that — with a blur. They can't see the details that God wants to show them. But when Rick put on his new glasses, he looked out that window and thought, *Those leaves have such details.* They'd always had those details, but he had never been able to see them until he received something that enabled him to *clearly* see.

This is what the Holy Spirit does. He comes to remove ignorance, and if you'll allow Him to work in your life, He will remove the blinders and open the veil. The Holy Spirit will show you things that God has planned for your life.

The Spirit of God Vividly Shows You Things To Come

There's one more Scripture that is important in understanding the Holy Spirit's role in unveiling God's plans. We find it in John 16:13. Here, Jesus described the ministry of the Holy Spirit, saying:

> **Howbeit when he, the Spirit of truth, is come, he will guide you into all truth: for he shall not speak of himself; but whatsoever he shall hear, that shall he speak: and he will shew you things to come.**

Notice that Jesus called the Holy Spirit "the Spirit of truth." When the Holy Spirit reveals things, you can trust what He shows you because He's the Spirit of truth. He will never lie to you or mislead you or deceive you. He is the Spirit of truth, and you can trust Him completely with every part of your life.

The word "shew" in John 16:13 is translated from the Greek word *anangello*, which means *to announce; to declare; to make clear*, or *to clearly and vividly portray*. It describes a *vivid showing or pronouncing of events*. The Holy Spirit wants to get so involved with us that He literally shows us things to come.

Somebody might say, "I understand He's going to show us things in the Scripture." And if you study the Scripture, there are a lot of examples about the revealing, showing ministry of the Holy Spirit. For example, in

Matthew 24, under the inspiration of the Holy Spirit, Jesus prophesied about end-time events as the Holy Spirit began to show things to come. (You can read more about it in Rick's book, *Signs You'll See Just Before Jesus Comes.*)

In Second Timothy 3, the apostle Paul described events that will occur in society at the very end of the age. This description is explicit and vivid. (You can read about this in Rick's teaching series, *Last Days Survival Guide.*) And the book of Revelation shows the Holy Spirit vividly describing events that will happen in the future.

The Holy Spirit Leads You *Personally*

The Holy Spirit will also speak to us *on a personal level.* You might say, "Will He *really?*" Yes! He cares about you. He cares about your future. He cares about your finances and your health. *The Holy Spirit cares about you.* If you will listen to Him, He'll show you what to do with your money. He'll even show you where or where not to go.

On the program, Rick shared a personal example of the Holy Spirit's vivid, caring guidance. By following the Holy Spirit, Rick and his family were protected from destruction.

Many years ago, I was going to take my family to Sri Lanka for a vacation at the end of the year and the beginning of the new year. We were all so excited about it. We'd been making our plans. One day as I was praying, the Holy Spirit spoke to me and showed me *not* to go there. He didn't tell me why. I just knew on the inside of me that *we were not to go to Sri Lanka.*

I didn't want to tell my sons because they were really looking forward to it. And I know Sri Lanka sounds exotic, but from Moscow (where we live), it's not very far away. We had found an inexpensive place to stay, and we were quite excited. Yet the Holy Spirit was speaking to me and showing me, *Don't go there. Don't go there.*

I could have ignored that leading, and we could have gone, but I chose to obey and trust the Spirit of truth. So I pulled the family together and said, 'We're not going to go. I don't know why, but the Holy Spirit is showing me *we are not to go to Sri Lanka right now.*'

The boys said, 'Dad, we're glad that you obey the Lord. We'll just stay home, and we'll have a good time.' Some time passed. And the very day we were supposed to be in our hotel on the southeastern shore of Sri Lanka, we came home, turned on the news, and saw that a huge tsunami had hit that part of the world.

The tsunami was so huge, it devastated Indonesia. *The hotel we were supposed to stay in was gone.* It had been carried into the sea, and everyone in that hotel had died. If we had been there, we would have died as well. But the Holy Spirit is faithful to show us things to come. And because I was listening, we weren't there when that tragedy took place.

He Will Open Your Eyes Fully to God's Good Plans

The Holy Spirit has come to remove ignorance. He wants to pull the veil apart so you can see, understand, and fully comprehend all the marvelous things God has prepared for your life. If you listen, He will show you what steps to take and what steps not to take. All of this is a part of the Spirit-filled life.

This is so encouraging! When you live the Spirit-filled life and partner with the Holy Spirit, He shows you what you can't see by yourself — and He will even show you things to come.

STUDY QUESTIONS

**Study to shew thyself approved unto God, a workman that needeth not to be ashamed, rightly dividing the word of truth.
— 2 Timothy 2:15**

1. God has a plan for you *specifically*! Read the following verses and note how the Bible describes that plan.
   - **Psalm 139:16 (*AMPC*)** — "Your eyes saw my unformed substance, and in Your book all the days [of my life] were written before ever they took shape, when as yet there was none of them."
   - **Jeremiah 29:11-14 (*AMPC*)** — "For I know the thoughts and plans that I have for you, says the Lord, thoughts and plans for welfare and peace and not for evil, to give you hope in your final outcome. Then you will call upon Me, and you will come and pray to Me, and

I will hear and heed you. Then you will seek Me, inquire for, and require Me [as a vital necessity] and find Me when you search for Me with all your heart. I will be found by you, says the Lord...."

- **Ephesians 2:10 (*AMPC*)** — "For we are God's [own] handiwork (His workmanship), recreated in Christ Jesus, [born anew] that we may do those good works which God predestined (planned beforehand) for us [taking paths which He prepared ahead of time], that we should walk in them [living the good life which He prearranged and made ready for us to live]."

2. Do you struggle with life's decisions, such as who to marry, where to live, or which job to take? As we learned in this lesson, the Holy Spirit is here to remove ignorance. If we'll allow Him to work in our life, He will remove any blinders, open the veil, and reveal the plan God has prepared for us! Read the following verses and list three main ways you can submit yourself to His leading.

- **Psalm 16:11** — "Thou wilt shew me the path of life: in thy presence is fulness of joy...."

- **Proverbs 3:5-7** — "Trust in the Lord with all thine heart; and lean not unto thine own understanding. In all thy ways acknowledge him, and he shall direct thy paths. Be not wise in thine own eyes: fear the Lord, and depart from evil."

- **Romans 8:14** — "For as many as are led by the Spirit of God, they are the sons of God."

PRACTICAL APPLICATION

But be ye doers of the word, and not hearers only,
deceiving your own selves.
— James 1:22

1. In Colossians 1:9-14 (*NKJV*), there is a Spirit-inspired prayer you can pray if you want to know God's will for your life. You can personalize it by praying "that you may be filled with the knowledge of His will in all wisdom and spiritual understanding; that you may walk worthy of the Lord, fully pleasing Him, being fruitful in every good work and increasing in the knowledge of God; strengthened with all might, according to His glorious power, for all patience and longsuffering with joy; giving thanks to the Father who has qualified us to be

partakers of the inheritance of the saints in the light. He has delivered us from the power of darkness and conveyed us into the kingdom of the Son of His love, in whom we have redemption through His blood, the forgiveness of sins." If you are wondering what God's next steps are for your life, start by praying this prayer over yourself.

2. God wants you to see and understand the wonderful things He has planned for you, and the Holy Spirit is the revealer. We need to have ears to hear so that we can receive His revealing ministry. Get to a quiet place and take an honest look at yourself. Do you have ears to hear what the Holy Spirit says to you? Have you heard and obeyed *some* things He said, yet disregarded other things? With sincerity, ask the Holy Spirit to help you hear Him clearly and obey Him accurately.

LESSON 2

TOPIC
Is God's Insignia on You?

SCRIPTURES

1. **Ephesians 1:13** — In whom ye also trusted, after that ye heard the word of truth, the gospel of your salvation: in whom also after that ye believed, ye were sealed with that holy Spirit of promise.

2. **Ephesians 1:13** (*RIV*) — When you were placed in Christ, God stamped you with a special seal and embossed it so deeply that it cannot be broken, erased, rubbed out, wiped out, deleted or removed. That unbreakable seal is the Holy Spirit. Once you were stamped with Him, it meant you had God's approval. He examined the contents of your heart and found nothing flawed or inferior. And because everything was in order, He stamped you with the Holy Spirit, which is His seal of approval. Anyone who has this stamp is headed for special treatment. This seal means you belong to God and no one is to interfere with you as a "package." This "Holy Spirit stamp" means the postage is prepaid to get you all the way to your ultimate destination. That means you can be sure that once your journey with the Lord begins, you are going to make it all the way to where God wants you to go.

3. **James 4:5** — Do ye think that the scripture saith in vain, The spirit that dwelleth in us lusteth to envy?

4. **1 Corinthians 6:19** — What? Know ye not that your body is the temple of the Holy Ghost...?

GREEK WORDS

1. "sealed" — σφραγίζω (*sphragidzo*): pictures a seal placed on a package after the product has been thoroughly examined and inspected to make sure it was fully intact and complete (the seal was proof that the product was impeccable); the insignia of a wealthy or famous person that guaranteed the package would be treated with tender care; a seal that guaranteed a package would make it to its final destination

2. "dwelleth" — κατοικέω (*katoikeo*): a compound word made up of the words κατα (kata) and οικέω (oikeo); κατα (kata) means down, and οικέω (oikeo) means to live; as a compound, κατοικέω (katoikeo) depicts settling down into a new home and making oneself to feel comfortable there; a permanent resident into a new home and making oneself to feel comfortable there; a permanent resident

3. "temple" — ναός (*naos*): describes a temple or a highly decorated shrine

4. "lusteth" — ἐπιποθέω (*epipotheo*): a compound word made up of the words ἐπί (epi), which means over and is an intensifier, and ποθέω (potheo), which means to yearn; as a compound ἐπιποθέω (epipotheo) is an intense, excessive yearning for something

SYNOPSIS

When the Holy Spirit fills us after we are born again, we enter into the glorious experience of the Spirit-filled life. We are sealed by the Holy Spirit unto God, bearing His mark upon our lives and confirming that we are brand-new creatures, guaranteed to arrive at our destination. The Spirit Himself makes His home within us, re-creating our inward man into a wondrous temple fit to be the dwelling place of God. He has come to stay on the inside of us, and He longs for us to give Him more and more of our being. God sanctifies and equips us to arrive exactly where He desires us to go in life.

The emphasis of this lesson:

The Holy Spirit not only lives within us, but He yearns for a full, satisfying relationship with us. He has made His home within us and transformed us into a glorious temple where God can forever dwell. He longs for more and more of us, transforming us more and more as we live out God's plan for our life.

The Power of a Sealed Package

Many Christians don't realize that God desires us to live a Spirit-filled life. But when we understand the wonderful fullness that the Holy Spirit brings to our lives, it changes everything for us! He reveals God's meticulously laid out plans for each of us, and He even reveals things to come.

In Ephesians 1:13, the apostle Paul wrote one of Rick's favorite verses about the Holy Spirit and living the Spirit-filled life. This verse declares:

> In whom ye also trusted, after that ye heard the word of truth, the gospel of your salvation: in whom also after that ye believed, ye were sealed with that holy Spirit of promise.

The Holy Spirit is our seal, and He's earnestly yearning for us. Let's take a look at what that means by examining the meaning of the word "sealed" in Ephesians 1:13. In the Greek language, the word for "sealed" is *sphragidzo*, which depicts *a seal placed on a package after the product has been thoroughly examined and inspected to make sure it is fully intact and complete.* This seal was proof that the product was impeccable. Normally, such seals bore the insignia of a wealthy or famous person, which guaranteed the package would be treated with tender care. It affirmed who the owner was and guaranteed the package would make it to its final destination.

In Greek and Roman times (and this still happens in certain places today), if a package was to be dispatched to another location, it first went through a series of investigations to make sure that the contents were not flawed, broken, or shattered. Everything had to be in order. The sender would examine every single piece of the contents to make sure each part was whole and intact. The process of examining every little fragment of the content was extraordinarily important for the one charged with sealing the document or package.

Finally, if everything was deemed to be intact and impeccable, the sender would pour hot wax onto the package or onto the fold of the document and seal it with the insignia of the owner — *signifying everything was complete and perfect, and therefore it could be dispatched.*

This package was paid for with such an expensive postage that it *guaranteed* the package would make it *all the way to its destination.* When people saw the insignia and recognized its owner, that seal was a signal to everyone: *Don't mess with this package because this package belongs to someone very, very important.*

You Are Sealed as God's Beloved Property

Let's take that historical insight into Ephesians 1:13, which says, "…ye were sealed with that Holy Spirit of promise." Here's what that word "sealed" means for *your* life.

After you believed and became born again, God *sealed* you with the Holy Spirit of promise. And the insignia on this seal He placed upon your life is important for several reasons. This seal bears the name of God Himself. The Holy Spirit Himself is the seal stating that you belong to God — and that people better not mess with you because *you belong to Him.* Wow!

No one would dare break such an insignia or disturb the contents, especially if the owner was a high-ranking individual. Likewise, when we have received the insignia, the impression, the seal of the Holy Spirit upon us, it is an alert that no one is to trifle with us. Friend, this is so very powerful.

You're Guaranteed To Arrive at Your Ultimate Destination

After factoring in the original Greek meaning of this passage, the *Renner Interpretive Version (RIV)* of Ephesians 1:13 says:

When you were placed in Christ, God stamped you with a special seal and embossed it so deeply that it cannot be broken, erased, rubbed out, wiped out, deleted or removed. That unbreakable seal is the Holy Spirit. Once you were stamped with Him, it meant you had God's approval. He examined the contents of your heart and found nothing flawed or inferior. And because everything was in order, He stamped you with the Holy Spirit, which is His seal of approval. Anyone who has

this stamp is headed for special treatment. This seal means you belong to God and no one is to interfere with you as a "package." This "Holy Spirit stamp" means the postage is prepaid to get you all the way to your ultimate destination. That means you can be sure that once your journey with the Lord begins, you are going to make it all the way to where God wants you to go.

In this interpretation, there are so many revelations. Some people see themselves as damaged, flawed products that God is trying to use. Not according to this verse! If you've been stamped and sealed with the Holy Spirit, then it means God looked at you, examined all the contents of your heart, your character, and your whole being, and called you whole.

It doesn't matter how broken, flawed, or messed up you were in the past. When you got saved, *you became a brand-new creature* — not a refurbished creature, not a fixed creature, not a better version of who you used to be. You became brand new! In fact, you were so impeccable that God sealed you with the Holy Spirit as the proof that everything was in order.

Sometimes you may feel that life is rough. You hit some bumps along the way, and you don't know if you're going to make it to where you need to go. But according to Ephesians 1:13, if you've been sealed with the Holy Spirit, that stamp means the postage is prepaid to get you all the way to your ultimate destination. You can be sure that once your journey with the Lord begins, you're going to make it all the way to where God wants you to go.

So instead of badgering yourself and beating yourself up, wrap your arms around yourself and declare, "I've been stamped with the Holy Spirit. That means everything is in order! No one is to mess with me — *including the devil*. When he sees the insignia of the Spirit pressed into my life, it is a warning that no one is to mess with this personal package. The postage has been prepaid to guarantee I'm going to make it all the way to the end." All of this is contained in that word "sealed," and there's such comfort in that.

God Came To Dwell Permanently on the Inside

When the Holy Spirit came into your life, not only did He come as a seal to guarantee that everything was in order. He also came to permanently dwell within you, which means the Holy Spirit is not a visitor. He is a *permanent indweller*. He came to permanently abide in you. This is evident in James 4:5, which says, "The spirit that dwelleth in us lusteth to envy."

The first thing this verse reveals is that the Holy Spirit "dwelleth in us." The word "dwelleth" is a compound of two Greek words — *kata*, which means *down*, and *oikeo*, which means *to live*. Putting these two words together, we get the compound Greek word *katoikeo*, which describes *settling down into a new home and making oneself to feel comfortable there.* It depicts *a permanent resident* — one who lives somewhere continuously.

When the Holy Spirit came into you, He didn't show up as a transient guest who was visiting and then leaving. The word "dwelleth" means your heart is not a hotel. Your heart is a *home!* And when the Holy Spirit came and did all these marvelous things within you — remaking you, washing you, and creating you brand-new — you became so fabulous on the inside that God said, "I want to live in there."

This is what happens in the new birth, and it's amazing! The Holy Spirit comes in and declares, "I'm going to live here." He settles down to permanently reside inside you. This agrees with what Jesus said in John 14:16 — that when the Spirit comes, He will "abide with you for ever." He doesn't come and go. He has moved in permanently.

When the Holy Spirit came into us at the new birth, He figuratively laid His own carpets on the floor, hung His own pictures on the wall, brought in a big easy chair, settled down on the inside of us and said, "I like it here. I'm going to stay." He settled down and made His home inside us.

He Transformed You Into a Beautiful Temple

The Holy Spirit made you His home, but really, He did much more than that. What else did He do? The Bible tells us in First Corinthians 6:19, "…Know ye not that your body is the temple of the Holy Ghost…?" The word "temple" is the Greek word *naos*, which describes a *highly decorated shrine.*

In Moscow, Russia, there are many magnificent cathedrals that are typical of a *naos* — *a temple.* They have vaulted ceilings. The floors are covered with precious stones. There is silver and gold. The decorations are amazing! These temples *dazzle* on the inside. That's what the word *naos* depicts.

When First Corinthians declares, "Know ye not that your body is the temple of the Holy Ghost," figuratively, it means the Holy Spirit came in to make Himself at home. He turned your interior into a cathedral so magnificent that God said, "I want to live there." And if you could see your interior, you would be amazed!

God Yearns To Have More and More of You

We've been sealed with the Holy Spirit and made brand new. The postage has been paid to guarantee we're going to make it all the way to the end. And not only that — the Spirit dwells in us. He's not a transient. He came to permanently abide within us.

But there's even more to the Spirit-filled life because James 4:5 declares, "The spirit that dwelleth in us lusteth to envy." What does that mean? According to this verse, the Holy Spirit dwells in us. And inside us, He is lusting. The word "lusteth" is the Greek word *epipotheo*, a compound word made up of the words *epi*, which means *over* and is an intensifier, and *potheo*, which means *to yearn*. As a compound, *epipotheo* is *an intense, excessive yearning for something*.

Usually, *epipotheo* is used in negative contexts to describe our yearning for sin or the things of the flesh. But in this particular verse, it is used in a good way to describe the Holy Spirit in us. According to James 4:5, when the Holy Spirit moved into us, He began to *yearn* for us.

In fact, this word "lusteth" is so strong that it could be used to describe a person who is addicted to drugs, and when the effect of the drugs wears off, he becomes doubled over, yearning for and desiring the next fix. This is a person with an obsessive yearning. He can never get enough. As soon as one fix wears off, he must have more and more and more.

We Are To Surrender Ourselves Completely

While the word "lusteth" is often used negatively, in James 4:5, it is used to express something positive. It tells us that the Holy Spirit not only came to dwell inside us — He *yearns* for us. He wants more of us every day — more and more of us. It doesn't matter how much we surrender to Him today. He's going to be asking for more of us tomorrow.

On the program, Rick shared an example from his own life of how wonderful it is to surrender all to the Holy Spirit:

> When I got saved at the age of five years old, I walked down the aisle as the church was singing the song, "I Surrender All." They sang, "All to Jesus, I surrender. All to Thee, I freely give." And I

surrendered my life. Do you know that was just the beginning? From that time until now, I've been surrendering my life to Jesus.

Every day, every week, every year, I find there's more of me that needs to be surrendered. And the Holy Spirit in me is not satisfied with the amount that I've surrendered to this point. He wants more. And tomorrow He's going to reveal more to me that I need to surrender to Him. This is such a divine exchange because as I surrender more of myself to Him, He fills me with Himself.

This is the process of *sanctification*. We surrender what He reveals to us that we need to surrender. We may not have even realized it yesterday, but today we see it. As we surrender that part of ourselves to the Holy Spirit, He fills that area of our life. And tomorrow, when we wake up and seek His face, He will show us something else that we need to surrender.

The Spirit in us wants more and more and more. He is fixated on us. He wants every part of us. He wants to fully fill us and fully possess us for Himself. All of this is a part of the Spirit-filled life that God has planned for us.

Trust Him With All of Yourself — and Allow Him To Fill Your Life

When we got saved, we weren't just a repaired broken object — we were *re-created*. In fact, our contents were so impeccable after the Holy Spirit came into us that God gave us the Spirit as a seal. The seal of the Holy Spirit means the devil is not to mess with us. It means we are impeccable on the inside. The postage has been prepaid for us to make it all the way to the end.

The Spirit of God has come as a permanent indweller. He's not a guest or a transient who's going to come and go. Your heart is not a hotel. It is a home, and He created inside you a cathedral. You are a walking cathedral. God wanted to live in you, and He does live in you.

The Spirit of God in you is yearning for you. He's saying, "Give Me more of yourself. Surrender to Me." As you make that exchange and surrender more of yourself to Him, He fills you with more of Himself — and this surrendering process has everything to do with the Spirit-filled life. He's pining for us. He wants more and more and more of us. Our job is to surrender to Him.

STUDY QUESTIONS

Study to shew thyself approved unto God, a workman that needeth
not to be ashamed, rightly dividing the word of truth.
— 2 Timothy 2:15

1. Ephesians 1:13 tells us that after you believed, "ye were sealed with that holy Spirit of promise." God sealed you with the Holy Spirit as the proof that everything is in order. How glorious! Now that you know what it means to be sealed, how does this affect the way you read and understand verses like Ephesians 4:30 and Second Corinthians 1:21-22?

2. First Corinthians 6:19 says, "Your body is the temple of the Holy Ghost...." You are magnificent on the inside! Read John 14:23, First Corinthians 3:16, and Second Corinthians 6:16. What else does the Bible say about God dwelling in you?

3. No matter how broken or how much of a mess you were in the past, when you got saved, *you became a brand-new creature.* You didn't become a refurbished creature or a better version of who you used to be. You became brand new! According to Second Corinthians 5:17, how many things have "become new" now that you are *in Christ?* Then read Second Corinthians 2:14; Philippians 4:13; and Philemon 1:6 (*NKJV*). What are some additional benefits to being *in Him?*

PRACTICAL APPLICATION

But be ye doers of the word, and not hearers only,
deceiving your own selves.
— James 1:22

1. When the Holy Spirit came into you, He didn't show up as a transient guest who was visiting and then leaving. As we learned in this lesson, the word "dwelleth" means your heart is not a hotel. Your heart is His *home!* And when the Holy Spirit came and did all these things within you — remaking you, washing you, and creating you brand-new — you became so magnificent on the inside that God said, "I want to live in there." Take some time to meditate on the fact that the Holy Spirit lives *in you* — permanently. Write down any insights you receive about this amazing truth.

2. The Spirit of God in you is yearning for you. He's saying, "Give Me more of yourself. Surrender to Me." As you surrender more of yourself

to Him, He fills you with more of *Himself.* This surrendering process has everything to do with the Spirit-filled life. He's pining for you. He wants more and more of you, and your job is to surrender to Him. Pray this prayer from your heart if you're ready to surrender more of yourself to Him and His plan for your life:

Holy Spirit, I surrender to You as You reveal the areas of my life that You want to take control of, which have been in my control until now. Help me surrender to You. And as I surrender to You, I ask You to fill me with more of Yourself and with more of Your power. In Jesus' name, amen.

LESSON 3

TOPIC

What If the Spirit Isn't Leading?

SCRIPTURES

1. **John 16:13** — Howbeit when he, the Spirit of truth, is come, he will guide you into all truth....

2. **1 Corinthians 6:19** — What? know ye not that your body is the temple of the Holy Ghost which is in you...?

3. **2 Corinthians 4:7** — But we have this treasure in earthen vessels....

4. **Ephesians 2:10** — For we are his workmanship, created in Christ Jesus....

GREEK WORDS

1. "temple" — ναός (*naos*): a temple or a highly decorated shrine; it presents the image of vaulted ceilings, marble, granite, gold, silver, and highly decorated ornamentation; pictures the most sacred, innermost part of a temple; the Holy of Holies

2. "guide" — ὁδηγός (*hodegos*): a derivative of the Greek word ὁδός (hodos), which describes a road; as the word ὁδηγός (hodegos), it describes a tour guide who knows all the roads; one who leads you on an excursion; a guide who knows the safest, fastest, and most pleasurable route to take

SYNOPSIS

Even the greatest shrines and cathedrals known to man, filled with precious stones, gold, silver, and extensive ornamentations, pale in comparison to the glory of the Holy Spirit living inside us! When we became born again, He transformed our inner man into a majestic temple in which God Himself dwells.

Not only does He live in us — He is also our expert guide, leading us through our entire lives. He knows precisely where we should go and what we should do in every situation. He is the Spirit of truth, the One we can completely trust to direct us. If we'll allow Him to be our guide, relying on Him rather than ourselves, He will bring us along God's glorious path for our life.

The emphasis of this lesson:

Have you ever contemplated what it truly means to have the Holy Spirit living within you? You are a shrine — a living temple — that is indwelt *by God Himself*. You are a repository of the treasures contained in Him! He loves you, He makes His home within you, and He guides you through life as an experienced tour guide, directing you in exactly the way you should go. All of these blessings are glorious facets of the Spirit-filled life He has planned meticulously for you to live — *in Him*!

Realize That You Are a Temple

In today's lesson on the Spirit-filled life, we are delving into what it means to be a shrine for the Holy Spirit and how the Holy Spirit wants to guide us. Let's start with First Corinthians 6:19, which says:

What? know ye not that your body is the temple of the Holy Ghost which is in you…?

In this verse, the apostle Paul was writing to the Corinthian church. The original Greek language of the beginning of this verse conveys the idea, "Don't you understand? Have you not gotten it yet?" Paul was speaking to the Corinthians in this way because they were living far below who they were supposed to be. They were indulging in immoral sexual behavior, drinking, and sinning. Paul responded by essentially saying, "Why don't you get it? Don't you understand who's on the inside of you? What? know ye not that your body is the temple of the Holy Ghost which is in you…?"

The word "temple" in First Corinthians 6:19 is the Greek word *naos* — an important term that describes *a temple* or *a highly decorated shrine*. It presents the image of *vaulted ceilings, marble, granite, gold, silver, and highly decorated ornamentation*. It pictures *the most sacred, innermost part of a temple.*

The very word *naos* is used in the Old Testament Greek Septuagint translation to describe *the Holy of Holies*, which was simply magnificent. The Holy of Holies was where the Shekinah glory of God, or physical manifestation of God's presence, dwelled in the temple during the Old Covenant. Paul did not use the word *naos* to refer to a plain, drab, unadorned place of worship. He used the word *naos* to evoke a very specific image in the minds of his readers.

If You Think Cathedrals Are Impressive, Wait Until You See God's Temple in You!

Rick grew up as a Protestant who attended church in rather simple buildings, so when he was young, he didn't understand the concept of a shrine. If he wanted to see something that looked like a temple, he visited a Catholic church with vaulted ceilings, marble, and beautiful ornamentation. But today he lives in Russia, and all over Russia there are historic Orthodox churches that are breathtaking!

In Moscow, there's a great church called Khram Khristá Spasítelya, which means the Temple of Christ the Savior. When you enter its doors, you lose your breath because it is so magnificent! The sanctuary is filled with impressive columns, as well as floors that are made not just of granite, but all kinds of precious stones too. The interior is covered with silver, gold, and bronze as well as gorgeous icons and beautiful ornamentation. *It is majestic on the inside.*

In the city of St. Petersburg, there is another cathedral called Isaakiyevskiy Sobor (St. Isaac's Cathedral), and it is amazing. For 80 years, it was the central place of worship for the Orthodox church in Russia. You have to see its magnificence to believe it. When you enter St. Isaac's, you see figures covered in gold, columns made of lapis and malachite, the most striking stained glass, beautiful ornamentations, and dramatic paintings. Its ceiling is superb.

When the apostle Paul said that your body is the "temple" of the Holy Ghost, he used the Greek word *naos*, which described a temple like the great cathedrals in Moscow and St. Petersburg. And his readers could understand his meaning because the First Century was filled with pagan temples and shrines to a whole pantheon of gods.

For example, in the city of Ephesus, you would find the great temple of Artemis, one of the Seven Wonders of the Ancient World. This temple was spectacular not just on the outside, but on the inside as well. There was an impressive statue of Artemis, and in front of it there was a reflective pool. The temple's interior was covered with all kinds of stones, marbles, curtains, and draperies. In Athens, on the Parthenon, you could visit the great temple dedicated to Athena. Its exterior was exquisitely covered with reliefs and sculptures, and its interior was breathtaking.

Majestic temples such as these were found all over the pagan world in the First Century when Paul wrote First Corinthians 6:19. The Greek word *naos* describes all of these temples in the pagan world. The city of Corinth had many temples like these as well. So when Paul declared, "Your body is the *naos* — the temple — of the Holy Spirit," he was saying that *we are a walking cathedral.* That's who we are!

God Created an Exquisite Walking Cathedral — in *You!*

When you look in the mirror, you may not see yourself as a cathedral. In fact, you may see blemishes. You may notice everything that you wish you could change with makeup, plastic surgery, or weight loss. You might not like your hair or your wrinkles. You may focus on all your defects. But beyond the exterior, on the inside, God has made a place in you so magnificent that Ephesians 2:10 declares, "For we are his workmanship, created in Christ Jesus...."

God put forth all His creative powers to fashion *within us* a space so splendid that Paul called it *naos.* Within us, there is a shrine. We are walking cathedrals. And on the interior, we are filled with rich ornamentations. We have the gifts of the Spirit on the inside of us. We have the fruit of the Spirit on the inside. The character of Christ is within us, and so is the holiness of the Holy Spirit. There is a treasure in us, and in fact, we could say that "X" marks the spot.

When Rick was growing up, he often pretended that he and his playmates were pirates looking for a treasure, and "X" always marked the spot. Likewise, when we read Second Corinthians 4:7, Paul says, "But we have this treasure in earthen vessels," which means "X" marks the spot. The treasure is right here — *within us.*

What is this treasure? It's the presence of the Holy Spirit. And the Holy Spirit is *in* us! But for God to dwell in us, a space had to be created inside us that was worthy of His dwelling presence. Friend, God does not live in a hut made of mud. He doesn't live in a shack. He lives in the most glorious environment in Heaven *and in you* — because you are a walking cathedral.

If you could see what you looked like on the *inside*, where the Spirit of God lives, you would be stunned beyond speech. It would be the ultimate confidence boost to anyone who has a poor self-image, because inside you is highly ornamented. In fact, you're so embellished on the inside that God, by His Spirit, said, "I like that. I'm going to move in there." That is amazing!

The apostle Paul said that we need to understand this. He wrote, "Know ye not…?" He was asking them, "Have you not yet comprehended that your body is the temple of the Holy Ghost?" God not only inhabited the members of the Corinthian church — He came to live in you too. He created within you a place where the Holy Spirit was willing to dwell. You're a new creature. Everything in your interior is impeccable!

Trust Your Guide on the Inside

The Holy Spirit has moved into you — and He wants to lead you. *You have within you a Guide.* Jesus referred to this in John 16:13, saying, "Howbeit when he, the Spirit of truth, is come, he will guide you into all truth." In John 14, 15 and 16, Jesus calls Him "the Spirit of truth" three times so that we will understand *we can trust the Holy Spirit.*

Friend, the Holy Spirit will never mislead you. He will never misguide you. He's the Spirit of *truth.* Whatever He says to you, you can bank on it and believe it to be true. In John 16:13, Jesus declares, "Howbeit when he, the Spirit of truth, is come, he will guide you into all truth."

The word "guide" used in this verse is the Greek word *hodegos.* It is a derivative of the Greek word *hodos,* which describes *a road.* But when it becomes the word *hodegos*, it is no longer just a road, but it describes *a tour guide who knows all the roads*. It means *one who is ready to lead you on an excursion*. This guide knows all the roads and all of the information about the sights to see and what not to see. He knows the best route that will give you the most pleasurable experience. All of this rich meaning is contained in this word "guide."

The Value of an Expert Guide

Imagine that you are taking a trip to ancient Ephesus with Rick. (It would be hard to find a better guide for ancient Ephesus than Rick because he has been there so many times. He even wrote a book about it called *A Light in Darkness*.) When you arrive at ancient Ephesus, you see that the harbor is a magnificent manmade structure that could accommodate more than 100 ships at a time. Next, you disembark from your ship and walk through a beautiful harbor gate onto a long marble road that leads right to the center of the city.

As you follow the marble road, you pass the bathhouse and the place where slaves were sold. You proceed right past the beautiful roofs, porticos, statues, and places where people sold little idols of Artemis, who is the goddess of Ephesus. You pass one of the markets and a gymnasium. When you reach the end of the road, there in front of you is the ornate theater of Ephesus. If you turn left, you can take a road that leads you to the temple of Artemis. If you take a right, you will come across the temple of Nero, the marketplace, and finally arrive at the exterior of an exquisite library. And then if you turn left and climb up the hill, you will walk a very ancient road called Curetes Street.

Up that hill, you discover bathhouses and all kinds of impressive buildings, including an ancient hospital and the ruins of the ancient temple of Domitian. Finally, you enter the upper part of the city where you see the upper marketplace and the Bouleuterion, the place where all the rich people did their business.

Rick knows all these details about ancient Ephesus because he has been to the site of this historical city many times, and he wrote a book on this subject. He has *been there*, so he knows all the sights. He understands what's interesting to see, as well as what visitors may not care to hear about. He knows the best way to go and is even aware of where the toilets are — which is important because there's only one place to go to the bathroom in the whole site, and if you miss it, you're going to be in trouble.

If you want to have a good experience when you visit Ephesus, you need to have a good guide. You can do it by yourself, but if you choose to do so, you're going to get confused. You'll find yourself looking at something and saying, "I wonder what that is. Wow, that's very interesting. I wish I had somebody to tell me what that was." And when you're finished studying it, you're going to say, "Where do I go from here?" You won't know where to go.

You can meander here and there and walk all over the place. But by the time you get to the exit, you'll be hot and exhausted. Your feet and back will probably hurt because you've been walking on hard surfaces the whole way. By doing it on your own, your experience won't be very enjoyable. Of course, you'll exit at the right place, but the *way* you exit determines whether you did it by yourself or you had *a guide.*

The Quality of Your Life Is Determined by Whether You Follow 'the Guide' or Not

Let's take this new understanding of the Greek word *hodegos*, which means "guide," into the context of this verse in John 16:13. Jesus says, "Howbeit when he, the Spirit of truth, is come...." He's the Spirit of truth. He knows all things, and He will *guide* you as a *tour* guide "...into all truth." We all come into Christ the same way — through Jesus. We all exit in the same way — through death. And because we've made Jesus our Lord and Savior, we're going to Heaven when we die. But what happens between the beginning and the end depends on whether we did it by ourselves or we let the Holy Spirit be our tour guide.

If we want to, we can do it by ourselves. We can figure it out and make mistakes by ourselves. We can wander this way and that, try this and that, take shots in the dark, and wear ourselves out. And, ultimately, we're still going to Heaven. But the quality of Christian life you have will depend on if you do it by yourself or you followed your Guide.

The Holy Spirit has been sent to be a tour guide for you as a part of the Spirit-filled life, and He knows everything in front of you. He knows what's going to happen today, tomorrow, and next year. He knows the mind and will of God for you. Everything you're trying to figure out, He already knows!

If you're trying to decide what job to take, who to marry, where to go on vacation, or what to do with your money, He knows the answer to all of these questions. You can try to do it by yourself without His help, or you can invite the Holy Spirit to take you by the hand and guide you. If you will have ears to hear, and if you'll pray in the Spirit, which is a part of being baptized in the Holy Spirit, you'll become so spiritually sensitive that *you will hear the Holy Spirit tell you where to go.*

He'll tell you when to pause and when to move. He'll prompt you to speak and warn you when it's time to be quiet. As you listen to His leading, your Christian life will become a pleasurable experience. And it won't be because you were smart; it will be because you had a good leader — the Holy Spirit — who guided you along the way. That *belongs to you* as part of the Spirit-filled life.

STUDY QUESTIONS

Study to shew thyself approved unto God, a workman that needeth not to be ashamed, rightly dividing the word of truth.
— 2 Timothy 2:15

1. Read John 14, 15 and 16 and note how many times Jesus refers to the Holy Spirit as the "Spirit of truth." What does this tell you about the nature of the Holy Spirit?

2. Read Second Corinthians 4:7 and Galatians 5:22-26. What "treasures" are found in you because of the presence of the Holy Spirit within you? What other benefits are there to having the Holy Spirit living in you? List the verses that support your answer.

PRACTICAL APPLICATION

But be ye doers of the word, and not hearers only, deceiving your own selves.
— James 1:22

1. Read First Corinthians 6:19. The word "temple" in this verse is translated from the Greek word *naos* — an important term that describes *a temple* or *a highly decorated shrine.* When you look in the mirror, you may not see yourself as a cathedral. In fact, you may see blemishes and imperfections that you wish you could change with makeup, plastic surgery, or weight loss. Now that you have a picture of what Paul was

saying to the Corinthian church, how does this put into perspective your perceived imperfections?

2. When the Lord gives you direction, you still have a part to play. Have you ever wrestled with the temptation to do what *you* want rather than following the leading of the Holy Spirit? How did you overcome and yield to the Holy Spirit's leading rather than your fleshly desires? Have you ever learned the hard way that it's better to follow the Holy Spirit than your own plans? Did that make it easier the next time you were tempted to call the shots yourself? Read Psalm 127:1 and write down any fresh revelation you receive from this verse.

3. Did you know that when you face major decisions, it's important to increase your time spent reading, studying, hearing, and meditating on the Word of God? And it's equally important to pray out the plan of God in other tongues. Hold the direction the Holy Spirit gives you up to the Word and ensure they align. Read Psalm 119:105, Hebrews 4:12, and 1 John 5:7 (*NKJV*). According to these verses, why is it vital to spend extra time with God's Word when making important decisions?

LESSON 4

TOPIC
Where Are Divine Revelations From?

SCRIPTURES

1. **Isaiah 53:5** — …With his stripes we are healed.

2. **2 Corinthians 13:14** — The grace of the Lord Jesus Christ, and the love of God, and the communion of the Holy Ghost, be with you all. Amen.

3. **Ephesians 1:17** — That the God of our Lord Jesus Christ, the Father of glory, may give unto you the spirit of wisdom and revelation in the knowledge of him.

4. **Ephesians 1:17** (*RIV*) — That the God of our Lord Jesus Christ, the Father of glory, may give you special insight — I'm talking about wisdom that's not naturally attained. This is the divine moment when the curtains are drawn back, and you are supernaturally enabled to see what you could never see by yourself.

GREEK WORDS

1. "Father" — πατήρ (*pater*): a father or progenitor; one who begets
2. "give" — δίδωμι (*didomi*): to give; to hand something over completely to someone else; to impart; to bestow as a gift; to give into one's care
3. "wisdom" — σοφία (*sophia*): insight; special insight not naturally attained; wisdom; revelation
4. "revelation" — ἀποκαλύπτω (*apokalupto*): a compound of the words ἀπο (apo) and καλύπτω kalupto; the word ἀπο (apo) means away, and καλύπτω (kalupto) is the Greek word for a veil, a curtain, or a covering; as a compound, ἀποκαλύπτω (apokalupto) describes an unveiling; a sudden revealing; it refers to something that has been veiled or hidden, but then becomes clear and visible to the mind or eye
5. "communion" — κοινωνία (*koinonia*): a derivative of koinos (κοινός), which describes things that are common or mutually shared, such as property that jointly belongs to two or more people; when it becomes κοινωνία (koinonia), it can be translated as communion, fellowship, or partnership

SYNOPSIS

Through the Holy Spirit who dwells within us, we gain supernatural wisdom and revelation so that we can understand the things God has for us. The Holy Spirit reveals everything to us — from our state of sin and our need to be saved to our righteousness in Christ, the baptism in the Holy Spirit, the promise of physical healing, and more.

The Holy Spirit loves to show us these things because it is His desire to partner with us, to share rich communion with us, and to fellowship with us. While He walked the earth as a man, Jesus Himself had a deep connection and relationship with the Holy Spirit, who empowered Him to live righteously, perform miracles, and be raised from the dead. And we can have this same intimate, powerful partnership with the Holy Spirit!

The emphasis of this lesson:

The Holy Spirit is not merely a "presence" or a "feeling." He is the third Person of the Trinity, and when we are born again, He makes His home within us. He gives us supernatural wisdom and revelation that we could never find on our own, so we can effectively fulfill the plans God

has meticulously prepared for us. When we learn to partner with the Holy Spirit, it transforms our lives and equips us to live fully for Christ in every area of life.

A Spirit-Inspired Prayer for a Spirit-Filled Life

Did you know that you can develop a relationship and a partnership with the Holy Spirit? When you do, it will change your life! In Ephesians 1:17, the apostle Paul prayed a divinely inspired prayer for the church of Ephesus that you can pray over yourself every day. This verse declares:

> **That the God of our Lord Jesus Christ, the Father of glory, may give unto you the spirit of wisdom and revelation in the knowledge of him.**

We'll focus on several points in this verse. First of all, God is called "the Father of glory." The word "Father" here is the Greek word *pater*, which describes *a father or progenitor, one who begets*. In this verse, the apostle Paul declared that God, the Father of our Lord Jesus Christ, is the One who begets glory. He produces glorious experiences, and we have an invitation to have an experience with the glory of God.

Then the prayer goes on to ask that God "give unto you the spirit of wisdom and revelation in the knowledge of him." The word "give" in this verse is a form of the Greek word *didomi*, which means *to hand something over completely to someone else*. It could also be translated *to impart, to bestow as a gift*, and *to give into one's care*.

In this Spirit-inspired prayer, we see that God wants us to experience His glory. If you've never experienced the glory of God, you can pray, "Father, I want to experience Your glory. You are the one who begets glorious experiences. Beget one for me. Invite me into a glorious experience."

The Holy Spirit Offers Us Supernatural Wisdom and Revelation

According to Ephesians 1:17, God wants to impart to you "the spirit of wisdom and revelation in the knowledge of him." The word "wisdom" is translated from a form of the Greek word *sophia*. This word does not describe wisdom that you can gain by reading a book or going to school. Rather, it describes *wisdom not naturally attained*. It is *special insight*. God wants to give you wisdom that is not obtained through natural means.

The verse goes on to say that He wants to give you wisdom "and revelation." The word "and" could be translated *even*. God is telling us what kind of wisdom this is. It's not naturally attained. It's "even revelation." He's putting it on a supernatural level.

The word "revelation" is the Greek word *apokalupto*, a compound of *apo*, which means *away*, and *kalupto*, which means *a veil, a curtain, or a covering*. When put together, they form *apokalupto*, which describes *an unveiling* or *a sudden revealing*. It refers to *something that has been veiled or hidden but then becomes clear and visible to the mind or eye*. It literally means *to remove the veil* or *to remove the curtain so you can see what is on the other side*. It refers to something that was always there, but you could not see it because it was hidden for a long, long time. Then someone pulls the curtain apart, and what was once invisible to you suddenly becomes visible to your mind or eyes.

There are many things that we cannot know by ourselves — for example, the will of God. We can't know every detail of the will of God for our life unless it is revealed to us. It's there, but it's on the other side of the curtain, hidden from view. We are utterly dependent upon the Holy Spirit for everything in life.

The Holy Spirit is the *only One* who can open the curtain and reveal God's will to us. And He *wants* to do that! Rick shared an example on the program of revelation in action. He explained:

> One time I was in Jerusalem with my team, filming TV programs. Usually, when we film, I work very, very hard all day long. Then when I come back to the hotel in the evening, I sit in my room and work on my computer, editing programs and getting ready for the next day. It's very hard work. Because I was working so hard and was so focused during this particular trip to Jerusalem, I never thought to open the curtain in my hotel room.
>
> Finally, the last day came, and just before we walked out of the room and checked out of the hotel, I thought, *You know what? I've never even opened the curtain. I wonder what's outside my window.* I pulled the string on the curtain, and very slowly it came apart. Right outside my window all week had been the most magnificent panoramic view of the city of Jerusalem! And I never saw it because the curtain had never been opened.

That view had been there for me to enjoy, and I never enjoyed it because the curtain was closed. But when I pulled the string and the curtain came apart, suddenly what was on the other side became visible to my mind and to my eye. That's what the Bible calls "a revelation."

We Need Revelation To Be Saved

There are many times when we receive revelation in life. For instance, an unsaved person cannot see that he is unsaved. You can sit down and explain to a person that he is unsaved. You can even explain to him that eternity is in front of him, and if he doesn't make a decision for Christ, he will go to hell — but he won't see it. Unsaved people just can't see this by themselves. They don't understand the full impact of what you're saying *until the Holy Spirit gets involved.*

But when the Holy Spirit reveals it, suddenly the unsaved person can see what he never saw before. Once the Spirit is involved, he can see that he is a sinner, and that's when he becomes convicted of his sin. We can't understand sin without a revelation.

Did you know you can't understand that you're the righteousness of God in Christ without a revelation? On the program, Rick shared that he grew up in church hearing that he was the righteousness of God in Christ. But he never understood what that meant until one day he was reading the Scripture. He said, "It was like the Holy Spirit pulled that verse apart and allowed me to see that Jesus became sin for me, that I might become the righteousness of God in Him. I saw it. It was a revelation."

We Need Revelation To Receive the Baptism in the Holy Spirit and Healing

Understanding the baptism in the Holy Spirit is another facet of the Spirit-filled life that comes to us only through a revelation from God. And so is the healing power of God. Rick shared his own personal story of coming to understand the baptism in the Holy Spirit and healing. On the program, he said:

> I grew up in a particular denomination where we didn't believe the gifts of the Holy Spirit still existed. We thought that people who spoke in tongues had psychiatric problems. We thought that

whatever they believed, it was doctrinally off base and whatever they were pretending to have, they were just faking. We didn't believe in any of it. In fact, we *disbelieved* in it.

Then one day, I walked into a room where I heard someone speaking in tongues, and in that moment I was shocked. But even more than that, it was as if the Holy Spirit said, "Rick, I'm going to show you something." He began to pull the veil apart. And for the first time in my life, I could see that the baptism in the Holy Spirit was *real*. Believe me, I was so convinced otherwise that I never could have seen it on my own. The Holy Spirit showed it to me. That's what a revelation is.

We also disbelieved in healing. I had never heard of anybody who was healed when I was growing up. But then one day, I heard about Isaiah 53:5, which says, "With his stripes we are healed." And in that moment, it was as if those words jumped off the pages of the Bible and seized me. The Holy Spirit pulled back the veil and showed me that by the stripes of Jesus, we have been healed. We can be healed. It's God's will for us to experience health and wholeness. I saw it. It was divinely *revealed*.

When Paul said, "That God…may give unto you the spirit of wisdom and revelation," that phrase could be better translated, "That God…may give to you *special insight, even revelation*." Factoring in the original Greek meaning of this passage, the *Renner Interpretive Version* (*RIV*) of Ephesians 1:17 reads:

> **That the God of our Lord Jesus Christ, the Father of glory, may give you special insight — I'm talking about wisdom that's not naturally attained. This is the divine moment when the curtains are drawn back, and you are supernaturally enabled to see what you could never see by yourself.**

It is the Holy Spirit who pulls the curtains apart so you can see what you need to know. What do you need to know about your future? What do you need to know about your job, your marriage, your kids, your finances, or your health? What is it about the Scriptures that you're longing to better understand? The Holy Spirit is the one who controls the curtain. If you'll acknowledge your need for wisdom that's not naturally attained and ask Him for a revelation, He will pull the string, draw the curtain apart, and show you what you desire to see. He'll give you a revelation.

You Are Invited Into Intimate Communion With the Holy Spirit

The Holy Spirit in you desires to be your partner in life, and we read about this in Second Corinthians 13:14, which says:

The grace of the Lord Jesus Christ, and the love of God, and the communion of the Holy Ghost, be with you all. Amen.

This verse ends with "amen," which means, *so be it.* The word "communion" is the Greek word *koinonia*, a derivative of the word *koinos*, which describes *things that people have in common or are mutually shared, such as property that jointly belongs to two or more people.* When it becomes the word *koinonia*, it can be translated as *communion*; *fellowship*; or *partnership.* You could interpret this verse as *"the communion* of the Holy Ghost be with you," *"the fellowship* of the Holy Ghost be with you," *"or the partnership* of the Holy Ghost be with you."

We are to have *communion* with the Holy Spirit. We're to have *fellowship* with Him, just like we can have fellowship with any human being. The Holy Spirit is the third Person of the Trinity, and we can have fellowship with Him. The word *koinonia* also means *partnership*, which means the Holy Spirit wants to become our most important partner in life.

Jesus Himself Partnered With the Holy Spirit

Consider Jesus. According to Luke 1:35, Jesus was conceived in the womb of the Virgin Mary by the Holy Spirit. According to Matthew 3:16, Jesus was empowered by the Holy Spirit, just as we are empowered by the Holy Spirit. Matthew 4:1 tells us that Jesus was led by the Holy Spirit. In fact, He was so led by the Holy Spirit that He didn't make a move unless He was led by the Holy Spirit, who was His partner.

In Acts 10:38, Jesus healed people by the power of the Holy Spirit. Matthew 12:28 affirms that Jesus cast demons out by the power of the Holy Spirit. In Hebrews 9:14, we see that Jesus was lifted up and was crucified in the power of the Holy Spirit.

According to Romans 8:11, Jesus was raised from the dead by the power of the Holy Spirit. And as we see in Ephesians 1:19-20, when Jesus was seated at the right hand of the Father, the very first thing He did was *pour out the power of the Holy Spirit upon the Church.*

From the beginning to the end, we see Jesus and the Holy Spirit always together. And the Holy Spirit was not mysterious to Jesus, nor just a feeling. Rather, Jesus knew the Holy Spirit as the third Person of the Trinity, and He worked hand in hand with Him.

In fact, in John 5:30, Jesus said, in effect, "I do nothing on My own. I initiate nothing by Myself. I only do what I see the Father doing." It was the Holy Spirit who showed Him what the Father was doing. And it was the Holy Spirit who led Him in what to do.

You Can Partner With the Holy Spirit

If Jesus needed to be in partnership with the Holy Spirit, then we need to be in partnership with the Holy Spirit as well. Rick noted in his program that he has learned this personally through his ministry work on TV and in writing many books each year. He shared:

> What I am teaching you today is not theory. When I need wisdom and revelation, if I'm studying a subject or I need to make a decision, I know that I can't do it by myself. I need wisdom that is supernatural. I need "even revelation." And I will pause and say, "Holy Spirit, I need You to show me what I need to see. Show me from the Scriptures what I can't see by myself. Show me the decision that I need to make for our ministry. Show me what we need to do to be more effective."

> And the Holy Spirit begins to pull the curtain apart. He shows me what I could never see by myself, and suddenly I receive wisdom that's not natural. I see what to do. The Holy Spirit is my partner. I can't do what I do by myself. Believe me, I know who I am — and by myself, I wouldn't be sitting in front of a TV camera. This is because the Holy Spirit partners with me. He empowers me. He helps me. And my friends, it's not just for me. This is for all of us!

Second Corinthians 13:14 is a verse for all believers. It starts by saying, "The grace of the Lord Jesus Christ...." You're meant to know the grace of the Lord Jesus Christ. The verse continues, "...and the love of God...." You know the love of God because you encountered it when you were saved. Then the verse goes on to declare, "...and the communion of the Holy Ghost, be with you all."

Everybody who is born again is supposed to know the *communion* of the Holy Ghost. You could translate that as the *fellowship* of the Holy Ghost or the *partnership* of the Holy Ghost. You need to understand that the Holy Spirit wants to give you wisdom not naturally attained — even divine revelation.

The Holy Spirit wants to be the same kind of partner to you as He was to Jesus! Ask Him to be your partner today, and you can begin a wonderful adventure with the Spirit of God that's a part of the Spirit-filled life.

STUDY QUESTIONS

Study to shew thyself approved unto God, a workman that needeth not to be ashamed, rightly dividing the word of truth.
— 2 Timothy 2:15

1. When Jesus was seated at the right hand of the Father, the very first thing He did was *pour out the power of the Holy Spirit upon the Church.* How does this act of Jesus speak to you about the importance of receiving the baptism in the Holy Spirit? What changes do we see in the apostle Peter *after* he received the Holy Spirit and spoke in tongues? (*See* Luke 22:55-62; Acts 2:14-41.)
2. What does the Bible teach us about the will of God concerning healing? And what does the Bible say about the connection between God's Word and receiving healing? (*See* Psalm 103:2-5; Proverbs 4:20-22; 107:20; Isaiah 53:4,5; and 1 Peter 2:24.)
3. What does the Bible teach us about God's glory? (*See* Exodus 33:18,19; Isaiah 60:1,2; John 11:40; 2 Corinthians 3:18.) If you've never experienced the glory of God — and you want to — pray this:

   Father, I want to experience Your glory. You are the one who begets glorious experiences. Beget one for me. Invite me into a glorious experience. In Jesus' name, amen.

PRACTICAL APPLICATION

But be ye doers of the word, and not hearers only, deceiving your own selves.
— James 1:22

1. A practical application of this lesson can benefit you for the rest of your life if you'll make a habit of praying Ephesians 1:17-23 for yourself each day. You can expect revelation from God as a result of this daily prayer. If you're ready to start today, pray these verses over yourself by personalizing them. Here's an example of how to do just that:

   Father, I pray that You, the God of my Lord Jesus Christ, the Father of glory, may give to me the spirit of wisdom and revelation in the knowledge of You. I pray that the eyes of my understanding would be enlightened — that I may know what is the hope of Your calling, and what are the riches of the glory of Your inheritance in the saints, and what is the exceeding greatness of Your power toward me, as one who believes — according to the working of Your mighty power, which You wrought in Christ, when You raised Him from the dead, and set Him at Your own right hand in the heavenly places, far above all principality, and power, and might, and dominion, and every name that is named, not only in this world, but also in that which is to come. And You have put all things under Your feet and gave Jesus to be the Head over all things to the Church, which is His body, the fulness of Him who fills all in all.

2. The Holy Spirit wants to be your partner in life. He wants to be the same kind of partner to you as He was to Jesus! Ask Him to be your partner today, and you can begin a wonderful adventure with the Spirit of God. If you're ready to take Him up on partnering together, pray this with sincerity from your heart:

   Holy Spirit, I desire intimate communion and constant fellowship with You. I want to enjoy a partnership with You like Jesus did when He was on the earth. Thank You for this wonderful adventure with You that starts today. In Jesus' name, amen!

3. In this lesson, we learned that as Jesus walked the earth, He didn't make a move unless He was led by the Holy Spirit — His partner. In John 5:30, Jesus said, in essence, "I do nothing on My own. I initiate nothing by Myself. I only do what I see the Father doing." It was the Holy Spirit who showed Him what the Father was doing. And it was the Holy Spirit who led Him in what to do. What about you? Do you wait to make a move until you have a clear leading from the Holy Spirit, your Partner? Take time now to go to the Lord in prayer and ask Him to help you see what to do and hear what to say in your cur-

rent circumstances. He is ready to lead you in even the minute details of your life.

TOPIC

Is the Wind of God Moving You?

SCRIPTURES

1. **Genesis 2:7** — And the Lord God...breathed into his [Adam's] nostrils the breath of life; and man became a living soul.

2. **Acts 2:2** — And suddenly there came a sound from heaven as of a rushing mighty wind, and it filled all the house where they were sitting.

3. **Romans 8:14** — For as many as are led by the Spirit of God, they are the sons of God.

GREEK WORDS

1. "suddenly" — ἄφνω (*aphno*): describes something that took them completely off guard and by surprise

2. "there came" — γίνομαι (*ginomai*): suddenly or unexpectedly

3. "sound" — ἦχος (*echos*): describes a loud blast; a loud roaring or a loud sound; describes the violent roaring and overwhelming sound of the sea in the middle of a huge storm

4. "rushing" — φερομένης (*pheromenes*): a derivative of the word φέρω (phero), which means to be carried, borne, or driven

5. "mighty" — βίαιος (*biaias*): forceful; mighty; violent

6. "wind" — πνοή (*pnoe*): a wind so loud that one may be tempted to cover his ears from the overpowering noise of it

SYNOPSIS

We see the Holy Spirit's amazing, mighty power in action in the book of Acts, when He came in like a rushing, mighty wind on the Day of Pentecost. Much like when Adam was brought to life when God breathed into his nostrils, the Holy Spirit brings life into our being. And we can be led by Him into situations that advance His Kingdom on the earth. What a glorious calling we have as sons of God who are led by the Holy Spirit!

The emphasis of this lesson:

On the Day of Pentecost, the Spirit of God suddenly moved upon the 120 believers gathered in the upper room. The wind — the breath of God — came into that room, and they were all filled with the Holy Spirit. He came and transformed them. And that's what happens when the wind of the Holy Spirit breathes on *you*!

The Mighty Power That the Wind Contains

As we wrap up this series on the Spirit-filled life, we'll look as we always do at what the Bible has to say. The Bible tells us the Holy Spirit is like wind, and He wants to lead us. Let's go to Acts 2:2 and look at this glorious verse about the Day of Pentecost. It declares:

And suddenly there came a sound from heaven as of a rushing mighty wind, and it filled all the house where they were sitting.

Rick shared that when he reads this verse about "a rushing mighty wind," his mind always goes back to his childhood growing up in Oklahoma. There people are accustomed to a lot of wind because Oklahoma is in the middle of what is called "Tornado Alley." As a child, Rick loved tornado weather. Nothing thrilled him more than to look out the window and see the skies turning eerily green, which meant rough weather was on the way. He would run out on the back porch and fix his eyes on the sky, looking for low-hanging clouds and hoping he would see them spin and turn into a tornado.

During tornado weather, Rick's mother would call him inside the house. At times, she would take him and his siblings into the bathroom, shut the door, hunker down, and wait until the storm passed. If they heard the tornado sirens sounding, they knew there was a tornado nearby or the winds were really bad.

When the sirens stopped, they came out of hiding and went outside to see what things looked like. Sometimes they would see entire trees had been uprooted or there would be electrical lines laying across the street, sparking each time they touched because there had been so much damage from the winds.

Likewise, when Denise was a girl, her family had to go into their basement one time because a tornado passed right over their home. They watched as the insulation was pulled from the sides of the house as the tornado passed over. When they emerged from their hiding place, they discovered that the massive tree in their front yard had been uprooted and was lying on the lawn.

The Wind Brings So Many Benefits to the World

There's so much power in wind, and, usually, we think about how its strength causes destruction, as can happen with tornados. But if there was no wind in the earth, we would have many problems. Without the wind, the earth would be stagnant. The air would stink because of pollution and the decay that happens in nature. But the wind causes the air to move around so that we don't have a stagnant, stinking world.

Wind is so essential that there would have been no development of our current world without it. For example, if there were no winds, no exploration would have ever occurred before the creation of the steam engine. Before the days of the nuclear-powered engine, explorers had to depend on the wind to fill their sails. Ships couldn't move without the wind. If there had never been wind, there would have been no exploration.

If the wind didn't exist, there would be no windmills to produce energy. We would not have civilization as we know it today. We would be hundreds and hundreds of years behind. Wind is essential for progress to be made, and mankind has always sought to harness the power of the wind.

The Move of the Spirit Happened
Suddenly and Loudly

Wind can't be seen, but it can certainly be felt. In the same way, we cannot see the Holy Spirit. But when He moves, He is like the wind, and we can feel His movement. We can see when His divine power has been released. This is described in Acts 2:2, which says of the disciples in the upper room, "And suddenly there came a sound from heaven as of a rushing mighty wind...."

The word "suddenly" is the Greek word *aphno*, which describes *something that took them completely off guard and by surprise*. For 10 days, 120 disciples had been gathered together in the upper room, praying and waiting for the wind of the Spirit. And then suddenly, it took them completely off guard and by surprise. Sometimes that's how the Holy Spirit moves. He takes you off guard and by surprise.

The verse goes on to say, "Suddenly there came...." The phrase "there came" is a form of the Greek word *ginomai*, which also describes something that takes you *suddenly or unexpectedly* off guard and by surprise. So twice in this verse, we find this was a sudden, unexpected event. The verse states, "Suddenly there came..." — taking them off guard and by surprise — "...a sound."

The word "sound" is the Greek word *echos*, which is where we get the English word "echo." It describes *a loud blast; a loud roaring;* or *a loud sound*. It describes *the violent roaring and overwhelming sound of the sea in the middle of a huge storm*. Jesus used this same word in Luke 21:25 to describe the roaring of the sea.

If you've ever been near the sea, especially during a storm, you know it is so noisy that when the person standing next to you talks, you can't even hear what is being said. You have to yell at each other because the sound of the sea is so loud. This is the word used to describe what happened when the Holy Spirit suddenly moved on the Day of Pentecost. It was not a quiet affair when the wind of the Spirit began to move. It was a loud, boisterous event.

When the Holy Spirit Moves, He Releases Overwhelming Power

Acts 2:2 goes on to say, "And suddenly there came a sound from heaven as of a rushing mighty wind...." The word "rushing" is the Greek word *pheromenes*, a derivative of the Greek word *phero*, which means *to be carried, borne, or driven*. The Holy Spirit was moving. His wind was borne right into the upper room where the disciples were. It came rushing in, and it was loud.

And not only that! The verse also says, "as of a rushing mighty wind...." The word "mighty" is the Greek word *biaias*, which describes something that is *forceful*, *mighty*, or *violent*. It is not necessarily destructive, but something that is violent, powerful, and overwhelming.

When we put all of this together, we find that when the Spirit of God moved on the Day of Pentecost, He moved *suddenly*. And when He moved, it was so *loud* that it was like the roaring of the sea during a storm. It sounded *violent*. It was not truly violent, but so much energy was being released that the sound resembled something violent. The word "wind" is a form of the Greek word *pnoe*, which refers to *a wind so loud that one may be tempted to cover his ears from the overpowering noise of it.*

On the Day of Pentecost, the disciples were not sitting in the upper room with their hands clasped in their laps. No, they had their arms in the air, feeling the movement of the Spirit. They had their hands over their ears because they had never heard such a noise in all of their lives, and they couldn't escape it. That's why the rest of the verse says, "…It filled all the house where they were sitting."

There are people who like things to be calm and peaceful, and their idea of a movement of the Holy Spirit is when something sweet, quiet, and peaceful takes place. But when the wind of the Spirit begins to move, it is rarely quiet. It is usually a noisy, boisterous event. On the Day of Pentecost, it was no quiet affair. They were likely putting their hands over their ears because of how loud it was.

Just as the wind can move ships and all kinds of equipment that creates energy, the Spirit of God began to move in that room. He released His energy, which transformed those 120 disciples into a mighty army. *Wow!*

Through the Spirit, We Become a Mighty Army

Imagine a dead church for a moment. Dead churches have no ability to revive themselves. But when they call out to God and pray, suddenly the wind of the Holy Spirit moves upon the church. And this body of believers, which had been dead, can suddenly experience life as the wind of the Holy Spirit literally breathes life back into that church again. *And this can happen to you!* The Holy Spirit wants to blow life upon you and back into you.

Friend, even when all of our organizing is done and is nearly perfect, we still lack divine power. It is the wind of the Holy Spirit that causes an organization or a church to once again become alive with power. That's the job of the Holy Spirit.

As we consider the disciples on the Day of Pentecost, let's remember Adam when he was first created. In Genesis 2:7, we read, "And the Lord God...breathed into his [Adam's] nostrils the breath of life; and man became a living soul." Adam was perfectly formed, but he had no breath in his lungs. Adam lay there, and he was probably the most beautiful human being ever created. He was made by the hand of God Himself. But Adam was lifeless because there was no breath in his lungs.

Before the Day of Pentecost, the believers were in that upper room. The Church was perfectly formed, but it had no breath in its lungs. Then on the Day of Pentecost, the Spirit of God suddenly and unexpectedly moved upon them. The wind — the breath of God — came into that room, and they were all filled with the Holy Spirit. He came with *energy that transformed them into an army.* Friend, that's what happens when the wind of the Holy Spirit breathes on you.

The Leading of the Holy Spirit Brings About Amazing Miracles

The Holy Spirit also comes to consistently lead us. Romans 8:14 reveals, "For as many as are led by the Spirit of God, they are the sons of God." To illustrate how powerful it is to be led by the Spirit, Rick shared the following miraculous personal testimony on the program:

> Many years ago, when Denise and I and our family first moved to the former Soviet Union and I began our TV ministry, I had it on my heart to begin broadcasting the Bible and my program in a Muslim republic. You wouldn't think that would be the place to go and find favor. At the time when I wanted to go on the air there, this republic was at war with a neighboring republic. They were fighting and killing each other. I was waiting for the fighting to pause so I could get on a plane, quickly fly to that republic, and negotiate for TV time.

> People said to me, 'Rick, you shouldn't go. It's dangerous. You could be killed.' But I knew the Holy Spirit was leading me to do it. I knew that. And Jesus said in John 16:13 that He's 'the Spirit of truth.' We can trust Him when He leads us to do something.

The day finally came when the fighting stopped, and my associate and I quickly flew to that Muslim republic. When we got off the plane, because a war was in progress, the officials thoroughly interrogated us and examined us. Finally, they released us, and we went on our way to the national TV channel to negotiate for broadcasting time.

As we sat in the hallway just outside the TV director's office, fighting broke out. We could hear machine gun fire, and, suddenly, men with machine guns began running down the hallway of the television station all the way to the end where fighting erupted outside the door. There I sat while all this was going on, listening to the machine gun fire, waiting for my appointment to begin. The TV director's secretary came to me and said, "Would you like a cup of tea while you wait for your meeting?" I thought, *This is amazing. There's machine gun fire and fighting, and she's asking me if I want a cup of tea. I'm here to negotiate for TV time.*

When I went into that office and sat down with that TV director, guess what? The director was a woman — and it was very unusual for a woman to hold such a powerful position in Muslim society. But her heart just happened to be open at that particular moment. She said, 'Can you show me one of your programs? Let me see what you brought.' And the program that I'd brought was a series I taught on how husbands should treat their wives.

I did not realize, of course, that the TV director was having troubles in her own marriage. When she saw my program, she said, 'Do you have another one you can show me?' I showed her another one, and by the time I was finished showing those two episodes about how a wife should be treated, God had wrapped His hand around the heart of that TV director.

She looked across the table at me and said (and this was completely unlikely), 'How often would you like to broadcast, and what do you want to pay for this broadcast?' Rather than giving me her requirements, she asked me what I was willing to do. I was able to make a deal for the proclamation of the Gospel in that nation, which had never occurred before.

And it wasn't because I was so smart; it was because I was led by the Holy Spirit. People said, 'Don't go. You shouldn't go. It's dangerous to go.' But I knew the Holy Spirit was leading me.

Be Led by the Holy Spirit

Friend, the Holy Spirit wants to lead *you*. He is a divine wind. He wants to release power into your life on a daily basis. If you will listen to Him, follow Him, and allow Him to be the leader, the Holy Spirit will lead you right to where you need to be *every single time*. All of this is a part of the Spirit-filled life.

If you feel like your life has become stagnant, you need the movement of the Holy Spirit to come upon you. He'll remove all the pollution and stagnation, and He'll breathe energy into you. He'll cause you to move again by the power and Spirit of God. The Holy Spirit desires to move in your life *right now* like wind. He wants to supernaturally lead you, but *you must trust Him*.

Jesus said in John 16:13 that the Holy Spirit is "the Spirit of truth" because He wants you to know you can trust His leadership. Romans 8:14 says, "For as many as are led by the Spirit of God, they are the sons of God." It is God's will for all believers to be led by His Spirit — He wants to give you a *Spirit-filled life*.

STUDY QUESTIONS

Study to shew thyself approved unto God, a workman that needeth not to be ashamed, rightly dividing the word of truth.
— 2 Timothy 2:15

1. In this lesson, we learned about what happened on the Day of Pentecost when the gift of the Holy Spirit was given. What does the Bible teach us when people are filled with the Holy Spirit? (*See* Acts 2:4; 10:44-46; 19:6.)
2. In First Corinthians 14:18, the apostle Paul said, "I thank my God, I speak with tongues more than ye all." There is so much value in praying in the Spirit by speaking in tongues! Read First Corinthians 14:2-14 and Jude 20. What are the benefits of speaking in tongues?
3. In Genesis 2:7, the Holy Spirit breathed into Adam the breath of life and he became a living soul. Read Acts 2:17-21 and First Corinthians 2:4-5.

What happened to those whom the Spirit breathed into in the New Testament?

PRACTICAL APPLICATION

But be ye doers of the word, and not hearers only, deceiving your own selves.
—James 1:22

1. The baptism in the Holy Spirit is a free gift for everyone who has called Jesus Savior and Lord. You can receive the infilling of the Holy Spirit and step into the Spirit-filled life today! Acts 2:4 says, "And they were all filled with the Holy Ghost, and began to speak with other tongues, as the Spirit gave them utterance." (*See* Mark 16:17; and Acts 1:8.) If you would like to be baptized in the Holy Spirit and speak with new tongues, simply pray the following prayer and trust the Holy Spirit to provide you with the sounds and syllables for your new Spirit-language:

   Lord, I ask in faith for this free gift, and I receive the baptism in the Holy Spirit right now. Thank You for hearing me as I pray and for baptizing me in the Holy Spirit with the evidence of speaking with tongues — a new supernatural prayer language. In Jesus' name, amen.

2. It is the wind of the Holy Spirit that causes a church to once again become alive with power. That's the job of the Holy Spirit. And He wants to blow fresh life back into *your* church. So if your church is dead, or not as alive as it once was or could be, call out to God and pray! Then expect the wind of the Holy Spirit to move upon your church and blow life back into it!

3. John 16:14 (*AMPC*) beautifully describes the ministry of the Holy Spirit by saying, "He will honor and glorify Me, because He will take of (receive, draw upon) what is Mine and will reveal (declare, disclose, transmit) it to you." Now that you know more about the Spirit-filled life, how can you show how much you value the leading of the Holy Spirit in your own life? Purpose in your heart to treasure what He transmits, honor His leadings, and obey His prompting.

A Prayer To Receive Salvation

If you've never received Jesus as your Savior and Lord, now is the time for you to experience the new life Jesus wants to give you! To receive God's gift of salvation that can be obtained through Jesus alone, pray this prayer from your heart:

Jesus, I repent of my sin and receive You as my Savior and Lord. Wash away my sin with Your precious blood and make me completely new. I thank You that my sin is removed, and Satan no longer has any right to lay claim on me. Through Your empowering grace, I faithfully promise that I will serve You as my Lord for the rest of my life.

If you just prayed this prayer of salvation, you are born again! You are a brand-new creation in Christ! Would you please let us know of your decision by going to **renner.org/salvation**? We would love to connect with you and pray for you as you begin your new life in Christ.

Scriptures for further study: John 3:16; John 14:6; Acts 4:12; Ephesians 1:7; Hebrews 10:19,20; 1 Peter 1:18,19; Romans 10:9,10; Colossians 1:13; 2 Corinthians 5:17; Romans 6:4; 1 Peter 1:3

CLAIM YOUR FREE RESOURCE!

As a way of introducing you further to the teaching ministry of Rick Renner, we would like to send you FREE of charge his teaching, "How To Receive a Miraculous Touch From God" on CD or as an MP3 download.

In His earthly ministry, Jesus commonly healed *all* who were sick of *all* their diseases. In this profound message, learn about the manifold dimensions of Christ's wisdom, goodness, power, and love toward all humanity who came to Him in faith with their needs.

☑ **YES, I want to receive Rick Renner's monthly teaching letter!**

Simply scan the QR code to claim this resource or go to: **renner.org/claim-your-free-offer**

Connect

WITH US!